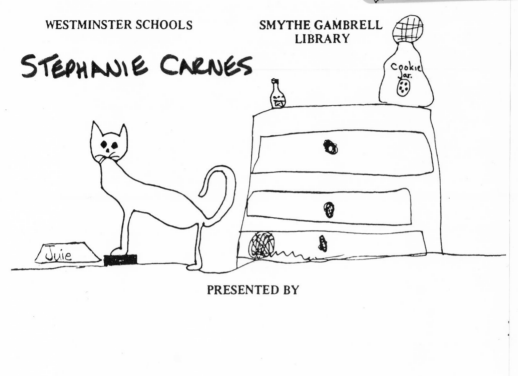

WESTMINSTER SCHOOLS

SMYTHE GAMBRELL
LIBRARY

STEPHANIE CARNES

Cookie
Jar.

Juie

PRESENTED BY

Messing Around with
**DRINKING STRAW
CONSTRUCTION**
A Children's Museum
Activity Book

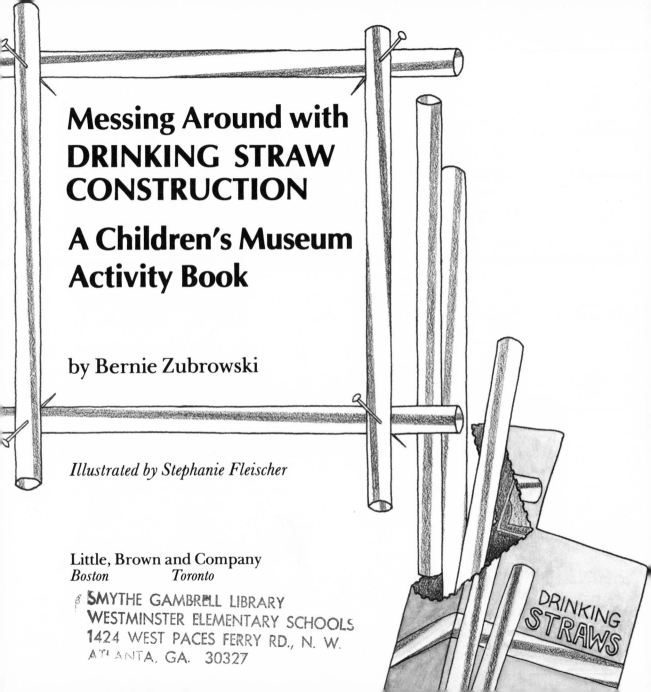

Messing Around with
DRINKING STRAW CONSTRUCTION

A Children's Museum Activity Book

by Bernie Zubrowski

Illustrated by Stephanie Fleischer

Little, Brown and Company
Boston   Toronto

FIRST EDITION

27305

Library of Congress Cataloging in Publication Data

Zubrowski, Bernie.
 Messing around with drinking straw construction.

 (A Children's Museum activity book)
 SUMMARY: Presents directions for constructing
simple houses, bridges, and other structures from
drinking straws. These projects illustrate funda-
mental engineering principles.
 1. Structural engineering – Juvenile literature.
 2. Engineering models – Juvenile literature.
 [1. Structural engineering. 2. Models and model-
making. 3. Building. 4. Handicraft] I. Fleischer,
Stephanie. II. Title. III. Series: Boston.
Children's Museum. Children's Museum activity book.
TA634.Z82   624.1   80-28164
ISBN 0-316-98873-1
ISBN 0-316-98875-8 (pbk.)

HOR

Published simultaneously in Canada
by Little, Brown & Company (Canada) Limited

PRINTED IN THE UNITED STATES OF AMERICA

To the children of Maseno School in Maseno, Kenya, who were great builders of model houses. May they also be as energetic and industrious in building a new nation.

BUILDING MODELS

We are surrounded by houses and tall buildings. Often we travel over bridges constructed in many different forms. All of these structures were built to be strong and last a long time. Craftsmen, engineers, and scientists over the years have discovered ways of making these structures strong. Some of the same principles were used in putting together the house you live in.

Have you ever thought about how houses are built? Perhaps you may have seen someone building a house in your neighborhood. You may have noticed that the wooden beams were placed in definite positions. In order to understand why this is done, the best way to find out is to build a house yourself. Of course, this isn't very practical. The next best thing to building a real house is to make a model. Often engineers and scientists build small models before the real construction takes place. They also test these models.

With a model, the results from the test do not necessarily indicate that the real thing will behave in exactly the same way. However, it does give some indication of what might happen.

The following pages show ways of making models of various structures. Building these models with some simple materials can help you understand how houses, tall buildings, bridges, and similar structures are put together.

BUILDING HOUSES WITH DRINKING STRAWS

In making models it is best to use a readily available material. It should be simple to work with and easily joined together. One such material is drinking straws.

Straws can be joined together in many different ways. For instance, by squeezing one end of a straw and placing it inside another, a longer one can be made.

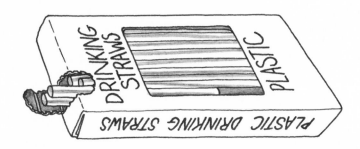

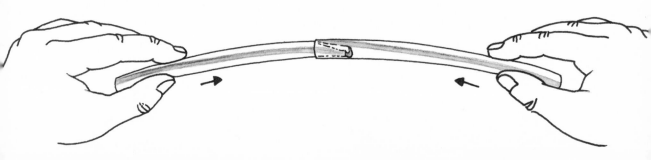

Pins or medium-sized paper clips can be pushed into the ends of the straws to join them together at the corners.

Straws can be put together with paper clips in the following ways:

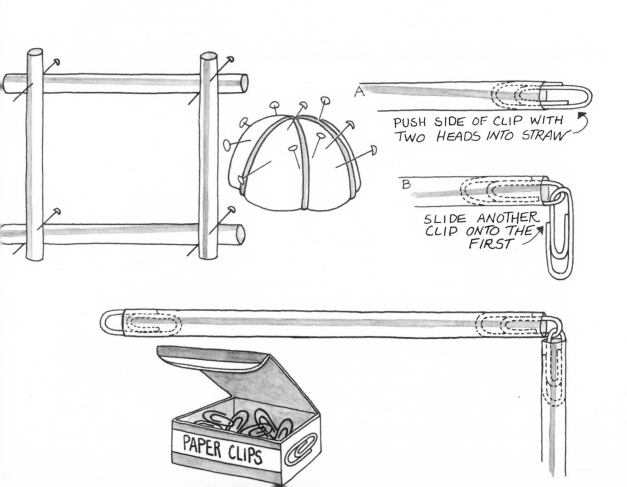

A

PUSH SIDE OF CLIP WITH TWO HEADS INTO STRAW

B

SLIDE ANOTHER CLIP ONTO THE FIRST

PAPER CLIPS

Putting Together
the Frame of a House

If you remove the shingles, bricks, or siding, most houses have a frame that looks like this:

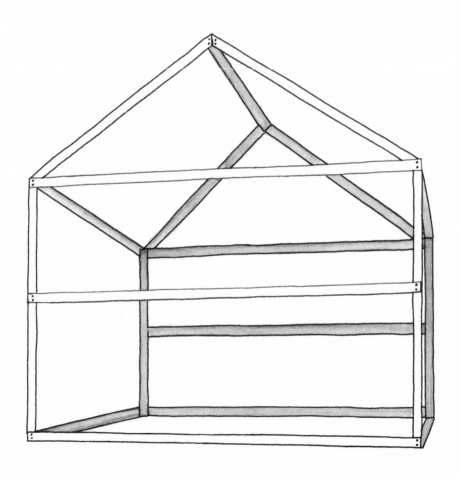

You can build a model house, using just one straw for each edge of the house. Making longer straws, as shown in the picture, can be more challenging. Also, when you are ready to test your model, bigger frames give more interesting results than small ones do.

When putting up a four-sided frame, you may discover that it does not stay up by itself. Someone has to support it. Try adding more long straws between the top and bottom of the frame and see if they help it stand up by itself.

Even when more long straws are added, as shown in the picture, the frame may still tilt.

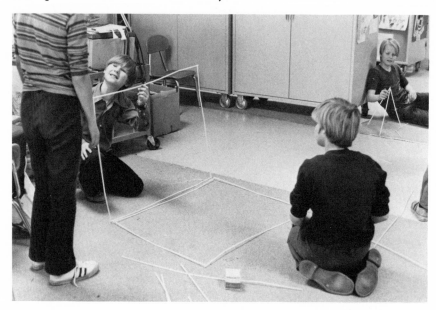

One solution is to pin the vertical straws to the bottom
of a piece of cardboard as these people did.

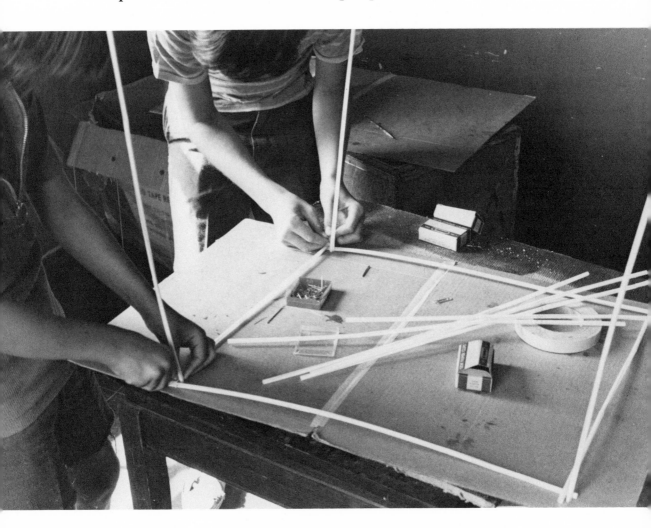

Another approach to this problem would be to consider just one side of the house. Make a square with the pins placed perpendicular (at right angles) to the square.

Where would you add one straw to keep the frame from moving to and fro? Is there more than one place where the straw would stop the motion?

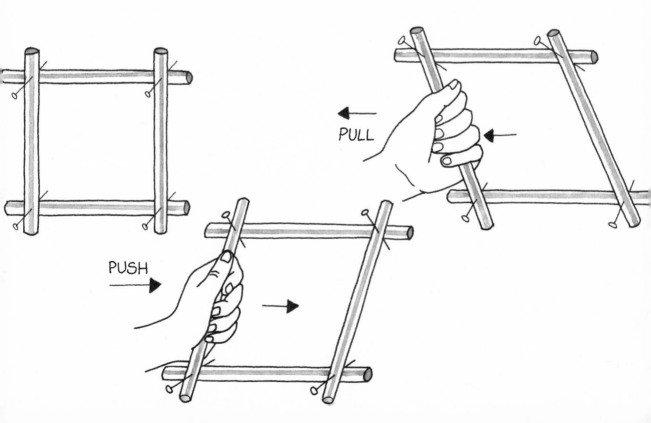

PULL

PUSH

Once you have discovered a solution to the preceding problem, you can try more complicated shapes.

What is the smallest number of straws and pins needed to stop each of the following from dancing or moving freely?

Save each figure you complete. Then compare them all and see if there is a general rule or pattern about how many straws are needed to stop any figure from moving to and fro.

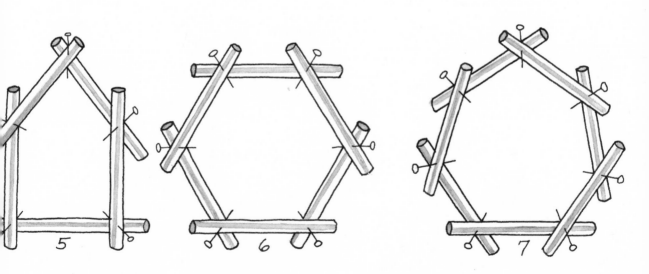

Examine each shape and note how many straws it took to make that shape rigid.

How many for the square?

How many for the pentagon?

How many for the hexagon?

If you have used the minimum number of straws and pins, there should be a pattern.

For instance, there is one interesting point you might have observed. Draw diagrams to show the smallest number of straws and pins needed to make the figures rigid.

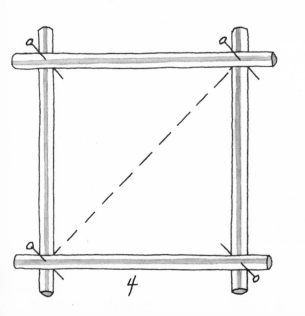

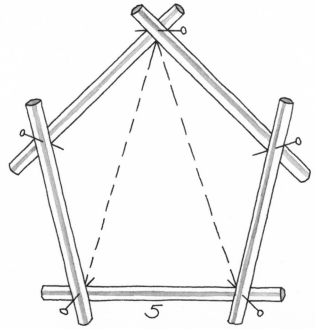

If you look closely, you might notice that each of the figures is now divided up into triangles. The square is composed of two triangles, the pentagon has three triangles, and so on. Can you predict how many triangles will be needed to divide up a seven-sided figure (a heptagon)? How many triangles would divide up a twenty-sided figure?

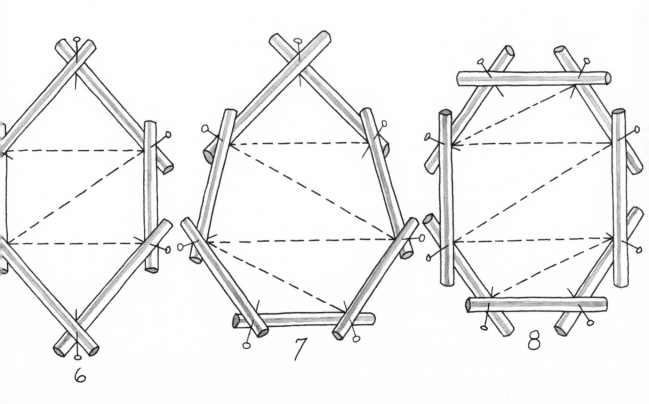

6   7   8

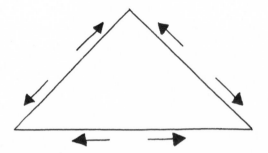

In all of these exercises the triangle shows up. The triangle is a very stable arrangement. When a force is put on a triangle figure, all the sides work together to hold it in place.

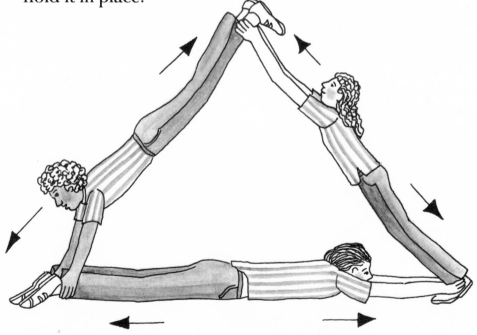

All the figures we've just mentioned were in two dimensions. Suppose you made a cube with one straw per edge. What would be the minimum number of straws added to the sides needed to make the cube stand by itself?

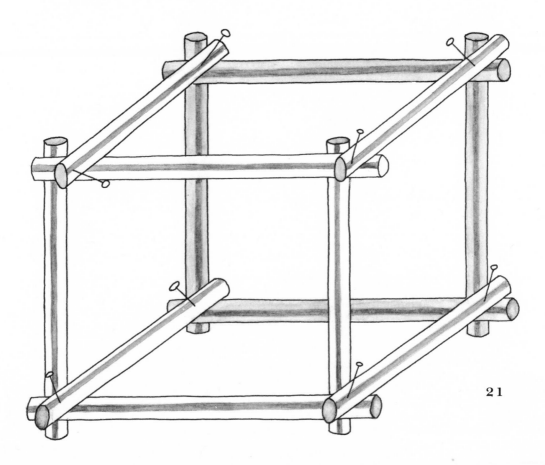

Making the Frame House Stand Up Itself

The previous activity returns us to the house we are building.

You've made the square rigid on one side of the house.

Does doing this help the entire house stand or only part of it?

What is the minimum number of diagonals needed to keep your frame up?

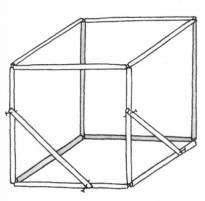

23

If you are lucky, there might be a house being constructed near you. If not, look closely at the photos below and the diagram on the following page. These are examples of how the frames of houses are usually put together.

24

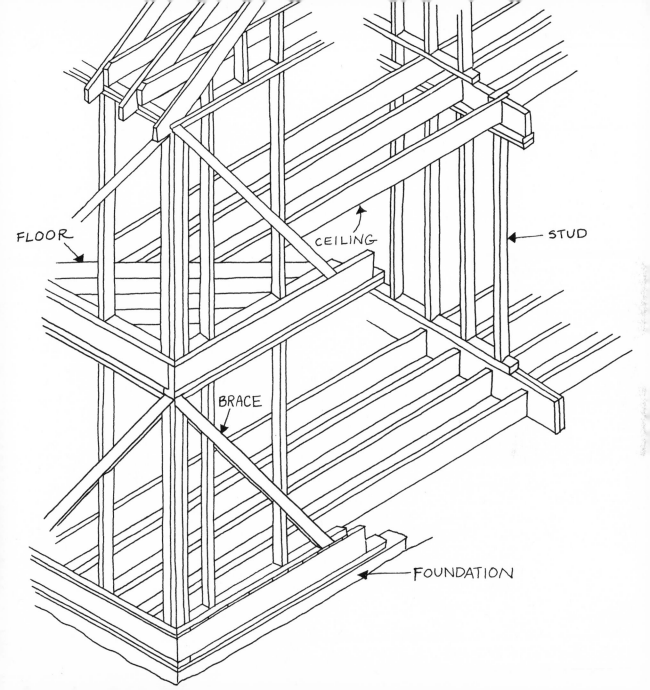

FLOOR

CEILING

STUD

BRACE

FOUNDATION

Compare your small framework with the ones in the pictures. Remember that both the pictures and the diagram show two-story houses.

Testing Your Model for Strength

Having built a frame that stands by itself, your next step is to test it. Where is it strong and where does it bend the most?

This testing can be done in the following manner. Place a hook on a juice can or paper cup and hang it somewhere in the frame house. Begin to put paper clips or small nails into the can.

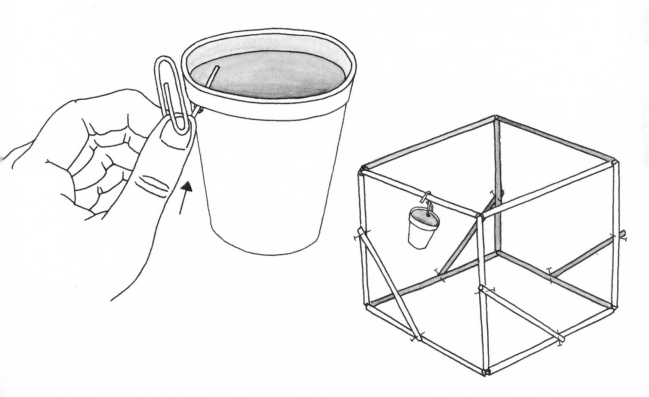

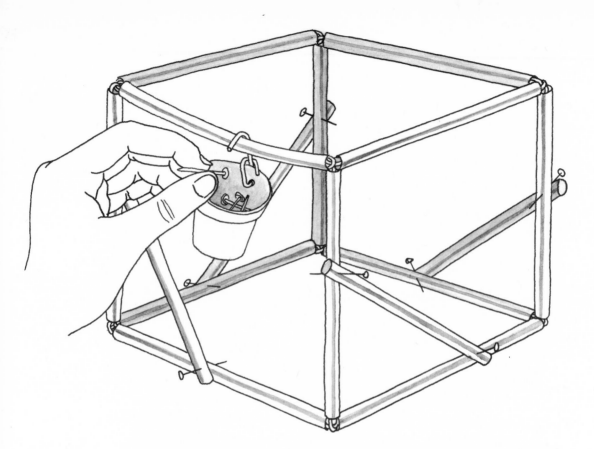

How many do you think you can add to the can before:

the frame bends a little?

the frame bends a great deal, but doesn't break?

the frame falls over or the straws break?

29

You may not want to break up your frame, but still you might like to test it. This can be done by adding nails to the can until the structure bends a lot. Stop adding nails and, with a yardstick, measure how far the can is from the floor. Make a mark on the stick to show the height of the can. Take the can off. Then place one or two long straws where you think they would stop the bending. Place the can at the same spot. Then measure to see if the new straws have given added support to the frame.

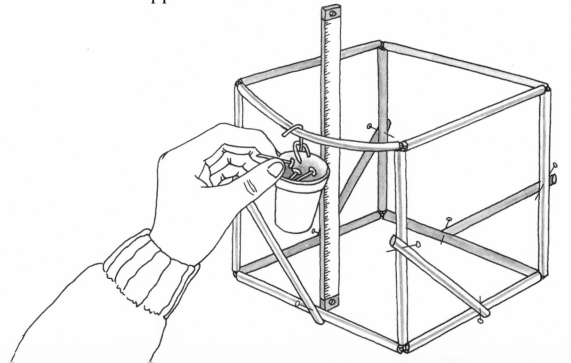

There are several points on the frame where you could place the can of nails for testing. One question you might consider is what part of the frame will support the most weight. Also, which part of the frame will support the least weight?

When a tin can of nails is added at the point shown by an arrow, the sides of the frame may bend. In which of the arrangements shown will straw sides bend the least?

Again, in each situation you can use the yardstick to measure the bending of the frame.

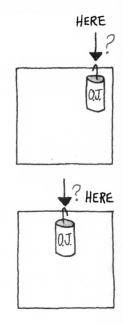

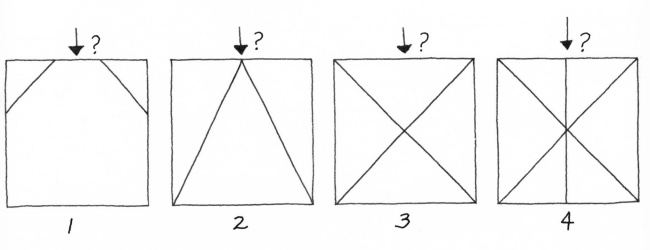

1   2   3   4

Go back to the diagram on page 31. Note how the sides are put together.

Which type of frame will support more weight?

Which arrangement will support the largest number of nails in the middle?

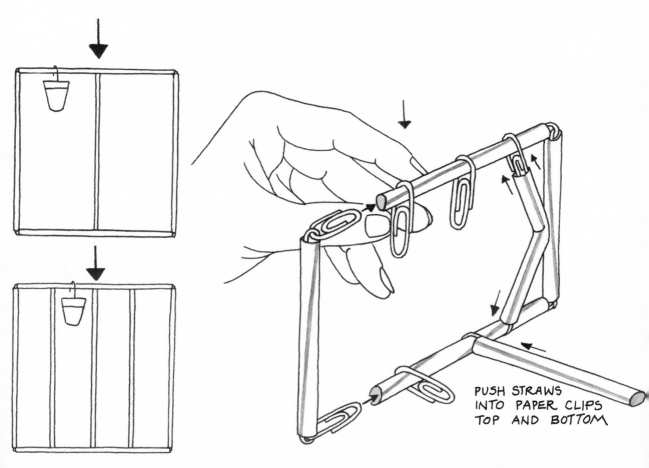

PUSH STRAWS
INTO PAPER CLIPS
TOP AND BOTTOM

Remember that in order to compare two different arrangements, the can must be hung in the same place for both. The weight should be added slowly to the can. When the straws bend to the point where they are about to break, you should stop adding nails. Then rearrange the straws or add more and follow the same procedure in determining the number of nails needed almost to break the straws in the second arrangement. You can then compare the two arrangements to see which is stronger.

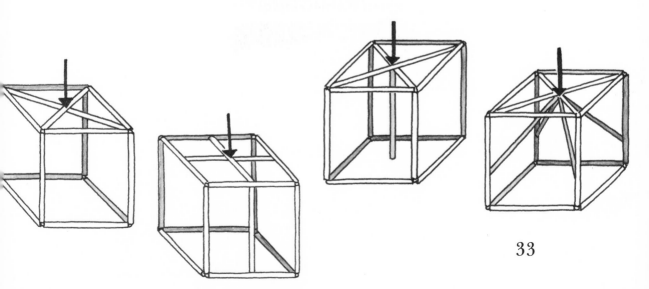

Comparing Rooftops

If you haven't already done so, you may want to add a roof to your structure. Look around your neighborhood. Are all the roofs the same shape?

There are many different kinds you can build. Can you guess which type of roof might be the strongest?

Here again you may have problems with your roof moving around and not being rigid. On the basis of what you did in the preceding activities and in testing your model, where would you put one or two straws to stop your roof from moving?

Suppose you were to make the following shapes:
Can these stand up by themselves?

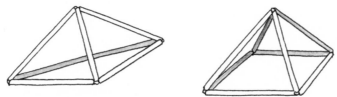

If you make the following, will it stand up by itself?

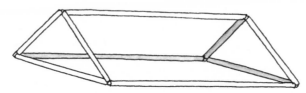

If not, how could you make it like the two above so that it will stand by itself?

Try testing various roof shapes for strength.

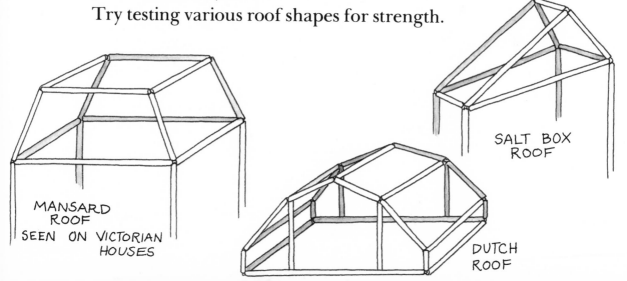

MANSARD
ROOF
SEEN ON VICTORIAN
HOUSES

SALT BOX
ROOF

DUTCH
ROOF

BUILDING BIGGER HOUSES

You may never be lucky enough to build your own house, but building a model house that you can crawl into or stand up inside in can do just as well. If you get enough scraps of lumber together, you can make a frame like the straw constructions. The following pages show one way of making a house big enough to stand up in.

Get together a lot of broomsticks from your basement and from all your friends. If you can't do this, go to a lumberyard and buy at least sixteen (more if you can) wooden dowels ¼ inch in diameter. To join these together, use old rubber tubing, garden hose, or rubber bands. If you use rubber bands, get a large box of thick ones. If you have several old bicycle inner tubes, you can cut these into small loops like rubber bands.

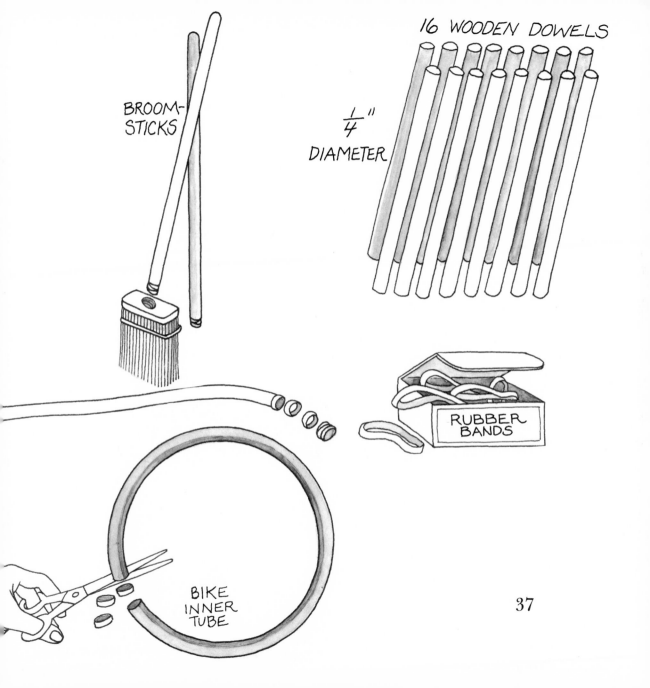

BROOM-
STICKS

16 WOODEN DOWELS

$\frac{1}{4}"$
DIAMETER

RUBBER
BANDS

BIKE
INNER
TUBE

37

With just the sticks and the rubber bands you can make a standing house as shown on the next page.

You will need to experiment to learn how best to wrap the rubber bands around the sticks so that the sticks stay together.

Here is one way of doing it:

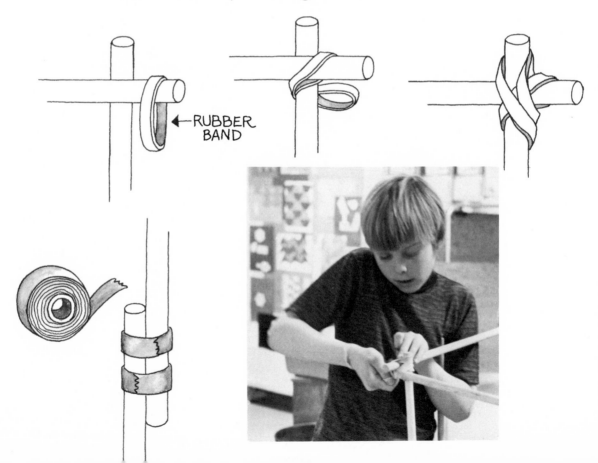

←RUBBER BAND

If you want to put together two dowels to make a longer stick, use masking tape as shown.

This house was built entirely of wooden sticks and thick rubber bands.

Besides walls, you could make your house even more complete. Gather together some batteries and bulbs. With these you can install lights in your house. With buckets, plastic tubing, and wire, you can set up your plumbing.

BRIDGES

As you already know, there are other kinds of frame structures. If you look closely at and study these structures, you may see similarities to that of the frames and rooftops of houses. Consider the many kinds of bridges you have seen.

Some of the earliest types of bridges were made from stone like the one shown below.

There were other early types, however, which were made from wood and looked like the following diagram:

This is not too different from the roof of a house as shown in the preceding pages. Perhaps you can apply your experience in testing rooftops to making a bridge from straws that is strong and rigid.

Start with a very simple bridge as shown in the drawing. How many nails can you add to the can before the bridge collapses?

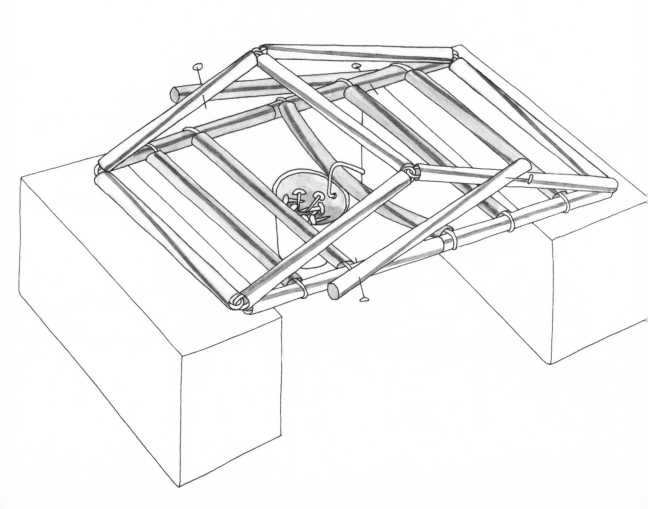

Make the same kind of bridge, but this time try adding a few more straws. Do these extra straws make the bridge stronger?

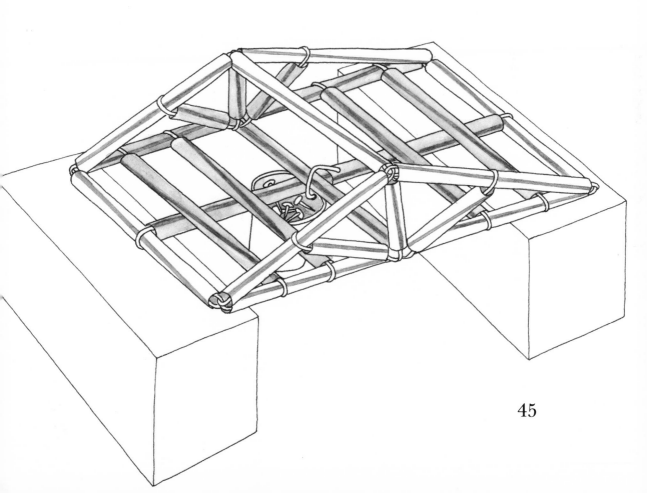

The structures you've just seen can be extended to span even larger gaps. This type was often used for railroad spans. The same arrangement has been used for rooftops in large buildings such as factories or sheds. Can you build a bridge like this that will span two or three feet?

How many nails can you put into the can hanging from the bridge before the bridge will bend a great deal or break? If a ruler is placed across the middle, as shown in the diagram, will the bridge hold a different number of nails?

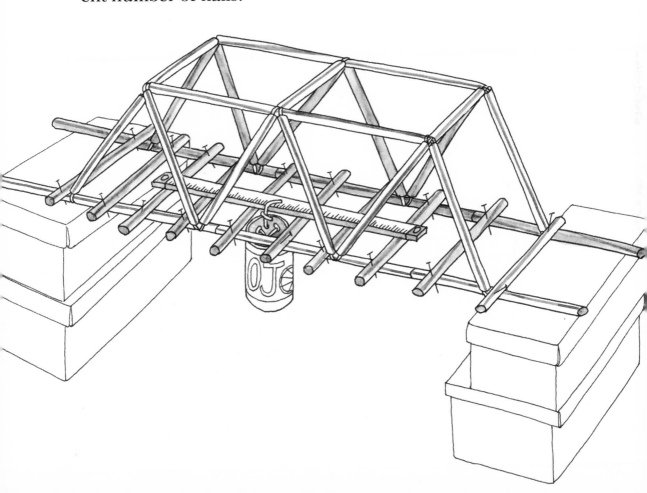

Building a Bridge You Can Walk On

As seen in previous pages, you can make a standing house using dowels or broomsticks and rubber bands.

Is it possible, using similar materials, to build a bridge on which you can walk?

At first you may think it takes hundreds of dowels to do this. Remember your experiments with the bridge of straws. With only a few straws the bridge could support many nails. With careful planning you might be able to make a strong bridge with only a few sticks. For instance, consider the sides of the bridge. If you are going to make a truss bridge, you can use something that is probably found around your house.

The type of rack shown in the drawing is used for drying clothes. It is made of only a few dowels and sticks and is light in weight. If you turn it on its side, you have an arrangement similar to a truss bridge. See if there is one like it around your house and if your mother will let you have it. If not, one can be bought at almost any department store.

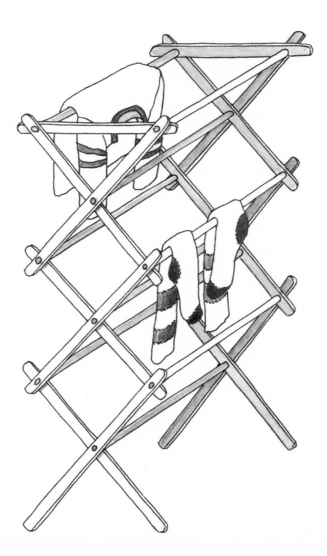

The rack should be reinforced in certain places to make sure it will hold lots of weight. Check the drawing to see how to do this.

BE SURE TO REINFORCE THE
TOP NOTCHED AND HINGED PART OF THE RACK.

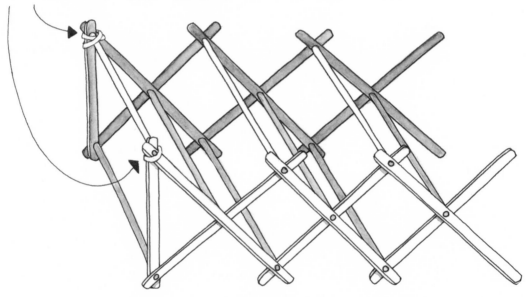

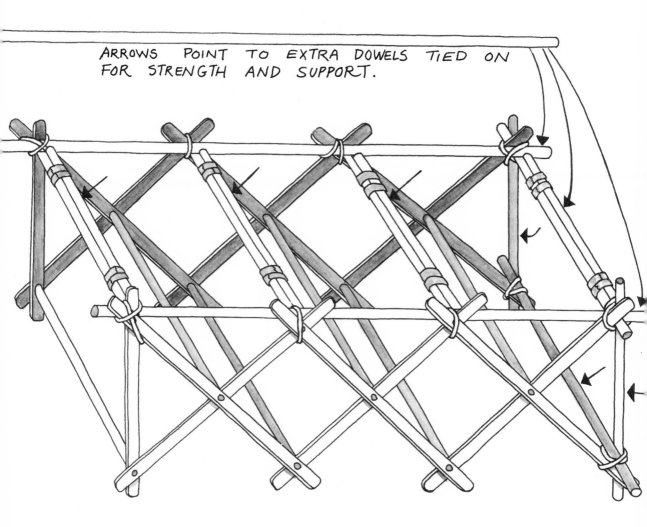

ARROWS POINT TO EXTRA DOWELS TIED ON
FOR STRENGTH AND SUPPORT.

51

You can place this structure on four chairs or four blocks. Make sure it is good and steady.

For the roadway you can use a piece of plywood or any other straight piece of wood. To make the bridge interesting, cut the wood so that it just fits over the frame. Also, try to get a piece of wood that is not too heavy. Tie this to the frame with rope.

To make sure the bridge is sturdy and strong, pile on buckets containing sand, or bricks or any other heavy objects you have lying around. Check to see if there is bending anywhere. If so, tie some more dowels at that point.

Then, with the help of a friend, try crawling across it yourself. As shown in the photo, this bridge can be strong enough to support a person. But treat this bridge with respect. It is not the kind to jump up and down on.

TALL BUILDINGS AND BRIDGES

In designing short bridges, engineers must consider the force of the structure's weight pushing down.

Another kind of force arises in the form of wind. If you have been out in a storm with the wind blowing very hard, you know what force the wind can have. Umbrellas can blow right out of your hand. The more surface exposed to the wind, the greater the force on the object. For instance, compare the force on an open umbrella to that on a closed one on a windy day. Small bridges are not much affected by winds. However, very long bridges, especially suspension bridges, are. In fact, one bridge buckled after it was built because engineers did not give enough thought to how wind affects long structures.

There is another kind of structure affected by the wind. Very tall buildings are pushed with a very large force when the winds blow. This force is one that could knock over a poorly constructed building. In designing tall buildings, engineers have had to think of new ways of making frames that would resist this type of force. What is interesting is that they have looked at how bridges have been built. Look at the following diagrams and pictures. Does the arrangement of certain parts of the frame look familiar?

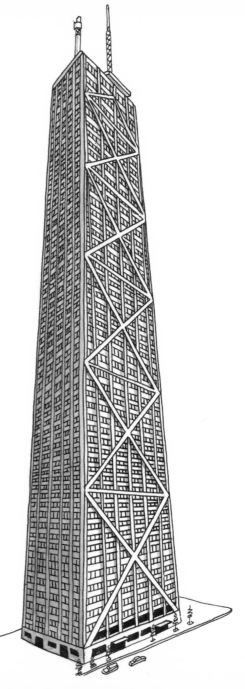

SEARS BUILDING
CHICAGO

Each frame of these buildings may be regarded as a bridge turned on end and fixed to the ground.

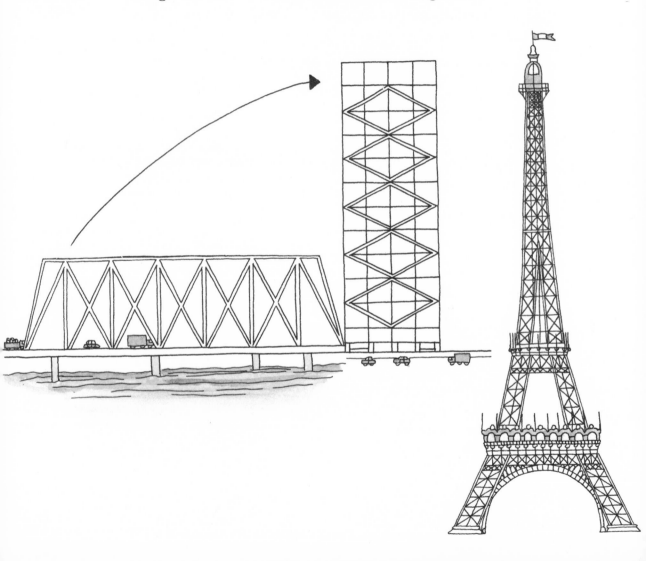

You may want to experiment with making tall structures using drinking straws. Here are some questions to consider.

How high can you build a tower of single straws joined to each other going straight up?

How high a pyramid-shaped tower can you make?

How high a tower can you make with the following kind of frame?

Start building a bridge like the one shown in the last section. Turn it on its side. How tall can you make this type of framework?

DIAGONALS AND TRIANGLES MULTIPLIED

You may have noticed that the shape of the triangle appears often in the framework of the different kinds of structures we have examined so far. The diagonal from the side of the house to the floor makes a triangle. Certain kinds of bridges could be thought of as a series of triangles arranged in a special manner.

In another section there was an exercise in making different shapes rigid. To make a square rigid, a diagonal can be placed from one corner to another forming two triangles.

Then a figure such as the hexagon could be made rigid by dividing it into triangles.

Also, in making all the other shapes shown on page oo rigid, the resulting frames were full of triangles.

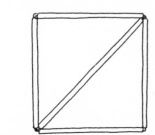

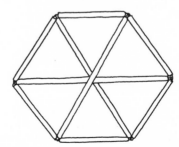

All of these figures are flat. They have length and width. What would a triangle figure be like in three dimensions? Would it also be rigid? Try making one with drinking straws and paper clips, and test it.

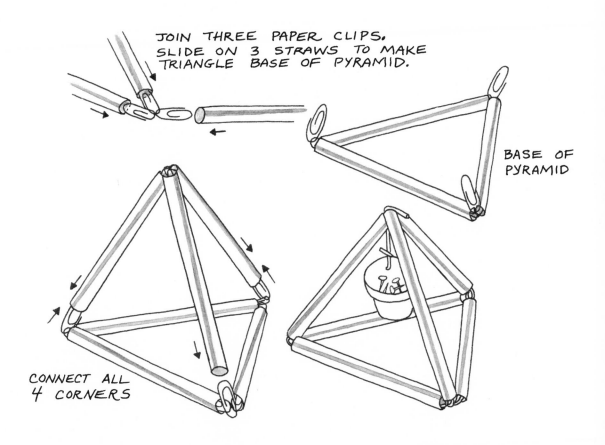

JOIN THREE PAPER CLIPS.
SLIDE ON 3 STRAWS TO MAKE
TRIANGLE BASE OF PYRAMID.

BASE OF
PYRAMID

CONNECT ALL
4 CORNERS

There are other ways of combining triangles and
making three-dimensional structures.

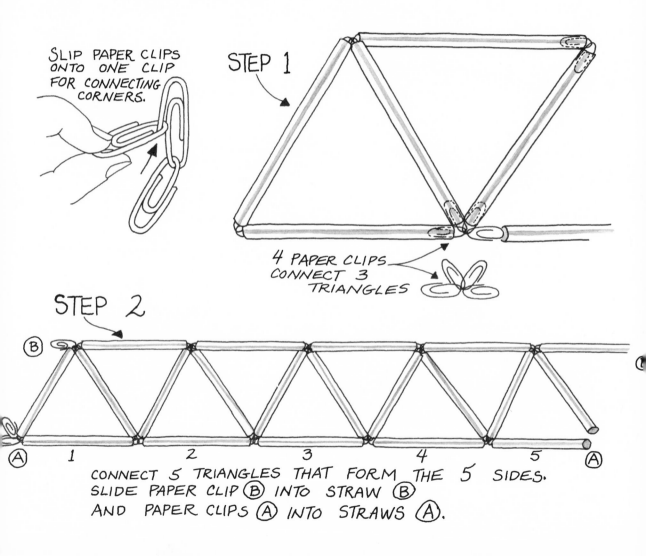

SLIP PAPER CLIPS
ONTO ONE CLIP
FOR CONNECTING
CORNERS.

STEP 1

4 PAPER CLIPS
CONNECT 3
TRIANGLES

STEP 2

Ⓑ

Ⓐ 1   2   3   4   5   Ⓐ

CONNECT 5 TRIANGLES THAT FORM THE 5 SIDES.
SLIDE PAPER CLIP Ⓑ INTO STRAW Ⓑ
AND PAPER CLIPS Ⓐ INTO STRAWS Ⓐ.

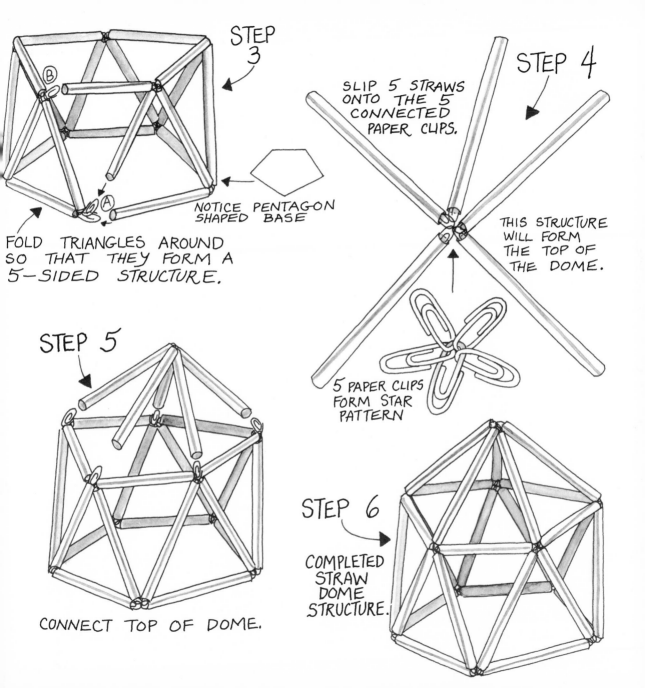

STEP 3

NOTICE PENTAGON SHAPED BASE

FOLD TRIANGLES AROUND SO THAT THEY FORM A 5-SIDED STRUCTURE.

STEP 4

SLIP 5 STRAWS ONTO THE 5 CONNECTED PAPER CLIPS.

THIS STRUCTURE WILL FORM THE TOP OF THE DOME.

5 PAPER CLIPS FORM STAR PATTERN

STEP 5

CONNECT TOP OF DOME.

STEP 6

COMPLETED STRAW DOME STRUCTURE.

These figures could be built not only with straws and paper clips, but it also could be made into a big structure, using dowels and rubber bands or garden hose.

FURTHER EXPLORATIONS

In this book we have explored ways of building a variety of structures. The same principle was used to make them rigid and strong. The triangle is a very stable arrangement and should be kept in mind anytime that you are building something. Some natural forms are also made this way. Look around you and see if you can find the other man-made things or natural objects that have triangles in them. Also, continue your model making and see if you can invent other structures that use the triangle.

SPACE FRAME
CEILING
IN SHOPPING MALL